Contents

Introduction

Some might say asylums kept the world safe from the most monstrous of people. Bleeding hearts would argue asylums were facilities with extremely inhumane ways of treating misunderstood health issues. As new atrocities enter our vision we tend to forget of the old. Just consider for a moment 9-11 and the current conflicts in Syria. Both incidents are horrifying and worthy of our disgust. Yet, if you follow history there are just as many horrific incidents, if not some that are even more so. Native Americans being killed for their land till nearly every tribe was wiped out. The mass killing of buffalo and the "inferior" mustang horses are just more of the inhumane things the human race is known for. Medical experiments on Americans to see the effects of mustard gas are yet another horrific event of history. So it is no surprise that taking a look at the history of psychology and the treatment options that evolved shows even civilized human beings were not all that ethical. In a world where we claim to be of high moral ground we are still capable of stuffing mentally ill individuals in places to be mistreated, experimented on, and in some cases, just a place to die neglected and alone.

Worse still, the person doesn't need to be diagnosed with a mental illness to die of neglect, without any family being there in the final moments. Nursing homes show plenty of evidence of neglect and mistreatment not only by staff members, but by family; in fact most cruelly by family who simply abandon the person as the family goes on with their busy lives.

It is no wonder we are at times fascinated with the horrors that have occurred because as humans we are able to say, "that won't happen to me" or "that's a world away and not something I should spend more than five minutes thinking about." When it doesn't happen to someone like a parent, child, or loved one, then it is fascinating to read of the horrors that psychological treatments have been advanced on.

Asylums are actually just a portion of psychological horror and unethical treatment the world is capable of. This book is meant to bring into focus the history of psychology and the various treatments humans have undergone when mentally ill. It is designed to make you think and wonder—what if someone didn't think of trephining. What if the first mental hospital never existed? What if a mental health professional didn't act like the angel of death? Would we truly have advanced in society without all the horrific events that took place? Is it possible to advance beyond the cruelty of the past to a more ethical future?

From the time of possession as the reason for behavioral illness to now, there is one thing that continues to remain unchanged despite how civilized we like to believe we are. Despite the fact that we are putting mentally ill patients in mental institutions more and more rather than prison with the general population, we are still very guilty of one thing. As you read you'll begin to understand what this one thing is.

Chapter 1: History of Psychology

Psychology, the soft science as many scientists refer to it, is one of the youngest fields of study the world has. This is not to say the notion of behavior influencing how people react is new. Even as early as Plato and Aristotle the concept of the mind being a major influencer on behavior has existed. If one considers Buddhism and the concept of enlightenment bringing a person to a different level of inner understanding, the idea of psychology has existed. Yet, it took until 1879 for it to be named as well as to become an academic discipline that would be taken seriously.

Wilhelm Wundt is credited with the first psychology laboratory and establishing psychology as an academic discipline at the University of Leipzig Germany. Despite his huge contribution to psychology most only remember Sigmund Freud and his theory of dreams, the ID, Ego, Conscience and Sub-conscience. Freud came a little later in the field, creating his psycho-pathology and psychoanalysis concepts in the later 1890s and early 1900s. Given how long it took for psychology to be considered an academic study, it is not surprising that inhumane treatment on a variety of levels occurred well into the 20th century.

The first concept of many psychological disorders was to consider the person to be possessed by a demon. It is not just behavioral disorders that became labeled as possession. Anthropological studies clearly indicate migraines, tumors, head injuries, and minor headaches were all considered to be possession. The more a person's behavior was "crazy" the more the belief of numerous cultures that the person was possessed by the most evil of beings, whether a demon or ghost. Studying the path of psychological treatment in terms of the first concept through to the inhumane treatments of the more recent past, is not only fascinating but it is also going to show just how scary a reaction to the unknown can be.

Psychological disorders including schizophrenia, psychopath, sociopath, psychotic, depression, bipolar, and any behavior that could make a person seem "crazy" was thought to be demonic or ghostly possession throughout the world and every culture would deal with the condition differently.

Trephining: A Neolithic Treatment

Trephining, according to archeological and anthropological research, dates back to the Neolithic time period or about 5000 BC. During several digs in the ancient world, trephined skulls were uncovered. The skulls had holes literally chipped into them with a crude stone instrument. It is believed that mental illness was the reason for the treatment, but in the eyes of the ancient people demonic possession, spiritual possession, sorcery, the evil eye or an angry god was the reason behind a person's strange behavior.

These cultures believed through the hole in the skull the evil spirit inhabiting the head could escape and thus leave the individual to be completely cured. Some of the skulls uncovered clearly showed the person did not survive. However, there are just as many hole-drilled skulls that show signs of the bone healing or calcifying around the wound. It is thought by most experts these individuals who healed probably suffered from a type of inter-cranial pressure that was "surgically" corrected by the hole being drilled and thus their change in behavior was "cured" as the ghosts or demons left. Migraines and skull fractures are typically the reasons for pressure inside the skull that could have led to extreme changes in behavior. Thus these individuals suffered the symptoms of mental illness, as we understand them today.

For centuries the Neolithic treatment of skull holes has existed. As the treatment continued into a more knowledgeable culture in terms of tools, better saws and drills for the purpose of trephining were created.

In the mid-2000s a report by anthropologists was aired on television regarding trephining. The report indicates certain cultures that have ancient ties to the world still use the process to rid people of demonic or spiritual possession. These cultures are cut off from the modern world, living mostly deep in jungles and they hold to their ancient beliefs of possession as the reason behind mental disorders in their people.

By the time Ancient Mesopotamia was founded, priest doctors began treating mentally ill individuals with magic-religious rituals. It is about this time that exorcisms, prayer, atonement, and incantations became the leading treatment for mental disorders. Sometimes punishment, bribery, threats, and submission were used as a means to get the person to act "cured."

Ancient China Takes a More Natural Course

Ancient China is the logical place to go after a discussion of trephining and demonic possession. An excerpt from a text written as long ago as 2674 BC or the 7th century BC stated an individual presented with symptoms of feeling sad, sleeping and eating less*. The person was showing excited insanity, but at times would become grandiose, exhibiting behavior like a noble and intelligent being yet at other times believing he could see god and the devil. The excerpt clearly indicates schizophrenia is a likely diagnosis.

*Note: the text origination date is unclear. Historians have a Chinese medical text thought to be written by Huang Ti in 2674 BC, but many now believe it was written in the 7th century and not by Huang Ti.

Unlike other cultures, the Chinese firmly believe in natural causes versus supernatural. They believe in Yin and Yang where the human body must be in balance. Therefore, when the human body is imbalanced there is a problem like physical and mental health illnesses. The Ancient Chinese remedy for Schizophrenia was to withhold food. It was felt the patient had too much "positive energy" from food and thus a decrease in the positive force would balance out the system. Starving a person for a few days is actually a rather mundane treatment when paired with other cultural concepts.

One thing must also be mentioned with regards to certain mental disorders. In some respects psychopathic symptoms were considered appropriate. This made it easier for psychopaths to actually hide their thirst for killing. Ancient times were what most consider uncivilized, where killing and war was a thing of necessity and great accomplishment. Today we consider those who continue to kill others in name of religion to be terrorists, while those who try to stop the killings are civilized. But that is a debate for another time. Early society, where war was considered a necessity of life, meant that warlords and generals could be psychopaths. Some of these men are referred to as bloodthirsty, but a look at their behavior in written records would have psychologists wondering if they were the first psychopaths.

Ancient Egyptians and their Advanced Thoughts

Egyptians, like Ancient Chinese, were more tolerant and forward thinking than other cultures. They considered treatment of behavioral related illnesses to be recreational activities like dances, concerts, and painting. By offering a sense of normalcy the person could relieve their symptoms and return to a normal state. Edwin Smith in the 16th century BCE is credited with detailing the brain and its mental functions. There is a papyrus document that indicates surgical operations, treatment of wounds, and identifies sites of mental functions within the brain.

Even with these cultures being more tolerant of mental disorders, there were just as many who could not believe in anything but the supernatural as the cause for mental breakdowns. Ancient Greece and Egypt both considered hysteria in women to be Conversion Disorder. It was known as the "wandering uterus", where the vagina needed to be fumigated in order to put the organ back in its proper location.

Early European Advancements

By the 5th and 3rd centuries BCE, European thinkers like Hippocrates were starting to make some conclusions about the mental condition being more natural and less of a possession issue. Hippocrates and a Roman doctor called Galen wrote many texts about natural causes. Galen was the first to state the four fluids of the body: bile, blood, phlegm, and black bile as the root of individual personalities. The concept was based on some of the similar thoughts of the Ancient Chinese and their belief of a balanced body being a healthy person in body and mind.

During the Middle Ages treatment was mostly about bringing equilibrium back to patients, such as using cupping and leeches to bleed out the imbalances for a healthy mind and body. Leeches and bloodletting was extremely common during these times as a way to correct any number of medical illnesses as well as psychological ones. Cupping is still a procedure used today, but it is more of a massage therapy than a medical or psychological treatment. A hot cup is placed on certain areas of the back as a method of treatment. Again it has to do with balance, where the Chinese would call it placement along the acupuncture pressure points. There is a five elements chart that displays the balance of the body, where these hot cups can be placed to stimulate the body as well as relax it.

During these advancements in the Middle Ages the concept of a proper diet to relieve "mad men" symptoms was growing. Those who would rave were given "cooling and diluting" diets, which mostly consisted of salad, barley water, and milk. Red meat and wine were taken out of the diet for these individuals.

Up to this point, most of these "crazy," "lunatic" or "raving mad men" were left to their families to take care of. Only when an exorcism, witch doctor, or trephining was necessary was outside intervention brought in.

Mistreating the Mentally Ill

The history of psychological treatment certainly shows that the mentally ill were greatly mistreated just in these few concepts. If you add in the stigma of having a mentally ill person in the family, then the cruelty truly begins. It is known particularly in Christian Europe that those suffering from a mental illness were abused, restrained, and caged. Some would be locked in cellars while others would be caged in pigpens. A few families would let the servants control the mentally ill person, but this could also mean extreme mistreatment such as leaving the person to be in their own waste, dirty, and unfed. A degree of these families with mentally ill individuals would just abandon them. If the person didn't die, then they would live by vagrancy, begging for whatever they could get or simply being pushed and mistreated until eventually death occurred.

This brings the discussion of the history of psychology in terms of the field of study and treatment, to the first mental hospital known as an asylum. The world of asylums was no better than the abandonment or restraints of a household, sometimes even worse than the concept of skull drills to relieve the sufferer of demonic possession.

Hollywood films showcasing the horrors of asylums in movies like Bram Stoker's Dracula, the House on Haunted Hill, and Shutter Island make the most out of the horror that was for some real life. The history of asylums shows the macabre treatments we are capable of, making humans suffer simply due to misunderstanding, stigma, and fear. In the next chapter you will discover that sometimes asylums where nothing more than prisons and certainly just a place to hide the mentally ill rather than provide proper treatment and healing.

Chapter 2: Types of Asylums

It is necessary to understand the definition of asylums in order to fully understand the different types. The dictionary calls asylums "establishments that exist for the aid and protection of individuals" who need assistance due to a mental illness, disability, physical handicap or persons who are not able to take care of themselves such as the elderly or orphans. This means, under the legal definition, an orphanage is an asylum. An assisted living facility for elderly care would also be an asylum since individuals living there may require full care or partial care.

When you look at the definition of asylum, it takes on a new meaning compared to the stereotypical insane asylum. When many hear the word asylum, they automatically picture a dark, dank place where the insane go to be treated. It helps that Hollywood has perpetuated this concept in horror films, and history shows have depicted what life was in early asylums, but many can also be a simple hospital, bright and sterile without the horror of unethical procedures attached.

What was originally called an insane asylum is now called a mental institution in order to be politically correct. They both mean the same thing—a place that has the custody and care of patients who suffer from mental disorders versus a location for medical care, a prison or orphanage.

Asylums can be public, private or state owned facilities. Public asylums usually allow any person with a mental disability to check in. They may receive some funding from state, but often there is a board of directors and shareholders. State run facilities are government paid for and available to ensure there are facilities for patients with mental disorders who may have limited funding or the resources to afford a mental institution. Private facilities are usually the most expensive type of care, with inpatient and outpatient facilities. Funding is often from charities, donations, and payments made by the patients. State run facilities can also be funded by charities and donations.

Asylums have been known by many names throughout history, from the first hospital to the current state hospitals. The politically correct term most people use today is psychiatric hospital, but mental hospital and psychiatric wards are also terms used frequently today. Psych wards or psychiatric wards are a sub unit of a hospital, which tend to specialize in serious mental disorders like clinical depression, manic depression, bipolar, psychopathic personality disorders, and schizophrenia.

Prior to this nicer term was the very horrible phrasing—lunatic asylum. In the 19th century the concept of lunatic asylums started to grow. Many felt it was the best way to house the "madness" of individuals. During the 19th century about two or three thousand lunatic asylums existed and by the beginning of the 20th century over 100,000 institutions were in operation.

Not all of the institutions were created equally. While some were designed for help and financial support, there were still many that were nothing more than a prison for the insane. Historical records show that some facilities would have male and female sides, where the insane were thrown into a few cells with no hygiene and just bread and water. Little was done to treat these individuals in the early insane asylums and most would never see the light or outdoors again. These prisons have given rise to the stereotype found in movies and TV.

Modern Facilities

Many of the early asylum buildings are still being used throughout the world. Some have been converted into other types of businesses, others into medical hospitals with psychiatric wards, and still many are current mental institutions. What has changed is our perception of care and treatment. A move of unethical treatment to ethical practices has corrected the problems generally seen in years past.

Modern facilities are outpatient and inpatient facilities. For the outpatient facilities, therapists are on staff to help talk, analyze, and create treatment plans for the patient to follow. Medications are still given to help patients who are suffering from self-harm, violence, or fear that they may eventually come to harm.

Mainly the patient is given a chance to be a part of their treatment and to seek treatment whenever they are in need of it.

When it comes to inpatient care there are a couple of options. Most of the facilities are going to have two different wards. The first ward is unlocked. The patient has the ability to leave whenever they wish; they can walk around the grounds, seek therapy, group therapy, and generally interact with other patients as a way of gaining treatment in a place of tolerance.

The idea is for the patient to feel comfortable and not worried about their care. This is much different than the asylums you will discover in the next chapter. The inpatient locked ward is still reminiscent of the locked facilities mental hospitals used to be. There is a need to ensure proper care for patients that can harm others or themselves if they are wandering about. There are also times that due to the mental illness the patient could wander off from the facility and end up hurt. For neglect reasons, locked wards are still available when the mental illness is severe. The change in modern facilities versus those in the next chapter is neglect.

Today, facilities cannot neglect patients like they used to. There are regulations in place to ensure it does not happen. This means proper hygiene is available. The advent of running water with indoor plumbing has also helped to a certain degree when comparing some of the original 19th century facilities.

The concept of padded rooms with straightjackets is largely gone which is also due to a change in regulations. Many states like Michigan do not allow patients to be restrained no matter the issue including self-harm. Rather patients in these situations are properly medicated to avoid injury, and all objects that could cause harm are not available.

Additionally, the staff to patient ratio is kept at a lower minimum to ensure that all staff members on duty can be aware of where patients are at all times. If they cannot, then there are at least measures in place to make it possible to look for the patient and do a checkup to ensure the person is still safe.

Unfortunately, no facility is 100% foolproof, so there are still going to be horror stories even with modern facilities. The goal has been to ensure that most of the issues and unethical treatment of the past is regulated so that it can no longer happen.

The First Asylum

Before moving in to the next chapter, mentioning the first asylum or mental hospital is a must. It is largely agreed that the first mental hospital was formed in Arabia, but the date is subject to debate. Some will say it was back in 700 BCE, while most consider the first mental hospital to be built during 900 AD in Baghdad. Other historians name a location in Valencia as the first site of a mental hospital. Unfortunately, we may never be able to discern the truth about the first asylum, but we do know that as far back as pre-history, or about 10,000 years ago, the idea of mental health care existed in terms of trepanning.

In the next chapter some of the most famous asylums are discussed as well as the idea or lack of treatment.

Chapter 3: Asylums Rather than Treatment

The Asylums chosen for this chapter are some of the most horrific. They are representations of the cruelty and chilling mistreatment of human beings the world has been known for. These locations were more a prison than a place for mental health treatment. One was even a location for a sideshow rather than treatment.

Bethlem "Bedlam" Royal Hospital

The Bethlem Royal Hospital was once called Bedlam by local UK residents and for good reason. It is perhaps the most famous of the lunatic asylums known for their lack of treatment. The London located asylum is the oldest surviving mental institution in the world. It opened in 1357. Living conditions in most lunatic asylums were deplorable with treatment either lacking or bordering on cruel. However, Bedlam was a special place for horrible and cruel.

It was a location the local community supported and many international visitors would ignore if not applauded. It was reported in several history books of the mental hospital that neighbors to the facility could hear roaring, crying, screeching, brawling, chains shaking, swearing, fretting, and chaffing. Whether this is just the imagination of those living close or true tales it is hard to know, but historically there is a record of the cruelty that happened in the hospital.

Those who managed the facility were known as the Keepers. Helkiah Crooke was one such keeper who ran the facility in 1619. Originally Helkiah was in the medical department for the royal household, but Crooke was called "unskillful" in medicine. It is assumed that Crooke was put in charge of the facility for his knowledge of medicine, and he was supposed to distribute medicine when needed to the patients housed in the hospital. Yet no records of any medical needs were recorded during the time he was in charge. Most of his notations referred to the patients as prisoners or the "poore." During his time at the helm, the conditions were never improved and no medical needs were seen to. Worse, for the 40 years in charge there was no inspection.

Part of the trouble arose due to insufficient funding. When an inspection was done, a request for new clothing and eating utensils was made, but that was one of only a few during the entire time the facility was open. It was run by the government, but lacked funds because families were meant to donate, which they did not.

During the 1500s and 1600s, when Bethlem Royal Hospital was certainly at one of its worst states, one has to remember that hygiene was different then. Showers or baths were not an everyday occurrence. Relieving themselves in the fireplace or on the street was common. But even with all that there was no reason for the people to be left to just die in the facility without treatment. Despite the poor conditions of the time period, why would anyone want to build a hospital over the sewer to have waste blocking the entrance as many horror stories tell?

One account of the hospital during the late 1500s states the water supply was provided by one wooden cistern in the backyard where the water had to come in by bucket. While chamber pots were in the rooms, they were rarely cleaned. In fact stories say patients threw them at staff, smeared the contents about the place or even tossed the pots out the window as people passed by.

Those with schizophrenia and other "disturbed" mentally ill were chained to the walls or to posts like dogs. Beds were only straw and the linens were never washed. Patients were always damp because the windows were exposed to the elements. While Crooke continued to run the facility the roofs caved in, the floors turned uneven and the walls started to buckle. Reports stated that residents went mostly unclothed and malnourished to the point of some starving to death. The idea was to deplete and purge the victims of their madness while also conserving costs of money.

Yet this is still not the most horrific part to Bethlem Royal Hospital's history. The hospital was first open to the public so they could bring food or money to see the sideshow. The public was encouraged to come see the patients in cages and in their rooms. Visitors would laugh as the insane banged their heads on walls repeatedly or as they poked them with sticks, or worse, threw things at the patients. The sideshows continued even into the 18th century. One wealthy, educated visitor said there is not a better lesson than to see the misery within the walls of the hospital. The visitor said it was a humbling experience and encouraged more people to go. The original building no longer stands. The hospital was moved in the 1930s to a new building in the suburbs. What was left of the original location was turned into a park. The central part of the building was reconstructed at the Imperial War Museum.

Metropolitan State Hospital

Moving across the pond, as the UK would say, is the next asylum with a chilling history. Metropolitan State Hospital in Waltham Massachusetts was established in 1930. It was the location for the Gaebler Children's Center, too. This abandoned facility is the site of some very horrific pediatric stories before it became a mental hospital. It is said that children were housed at the facility, but it was more like a prison. The children were sedated and disciplined to the point that it is said a child psychiatric patient died due to an accidental poisoning. It happened in the 1960s.

The 1960s is just the tip of the horror iceberg for this facility. The facility became nicknamed the "Hospital of Seven Teeth" in the 70s. Anna Marie Davee disappeared in 1978 when she went for a walk. In 1980 it was discovered that another patient, Melvin Wilson, killed her. Police were taken around by Wilson to three graves where he put parts of her body. The dismemberment was horrific enough, but Davee actually kept seven teeth as his souvenir. It shows that even in the late 70s proper treatment was not provided to patients and that the psychopath or sociopath, as Melvin Wilson may have been, could get away with killing someone for two years before the crime and lack of treatment was revealed. The hospital was eventually closed in 1992.

Danvers State Hospital

Danvers State Hospital was also located in Massachusetts. What makes this place different is the appearance of the building versus what went on inside. An older mental institution, it was built in 1887 to be a very pleasing gothic structure. Modeled on the Thomas Kirkbride concept of compassionate mental health treatment, the facility was ornate inside and out with private rooms, long wings, and plenty of sunshine. Of course, while the design was appealing that doesn't mean it was run as it was meant to be. It was built to house 600 patients, but by 1939 it was a facility overrun with 2,300 patients and a small staff.

Staff members were unable to keep patients clean or even under control because there were not enough of them. Stories of patients dying out of sight of staff also tell of the bodies being left undiscovered for days, with the corpses rotting in forgotten rooms. Slowly the introduction of straightjackets, solitary confinement, and electroshock therapy became the norm at Danvers State Hospital. It is said that Danvers is the "birthplace of the prefrontal lobotomy." In the 1940s, visitors described patients at Danvers to walk the halls staring vacantly. It might have been due to neglect or the medical treatments they had to undergo like lobotomies. By 1969 some of the hospital was closed off and starting to turn to ruins. In 1985, most of the facility was empty, and in 1992 it was abandoned, closed to rot like many of the patients that also rotted inside.

New Jersey State Lunatic Asylum

The New Jersey State Lunatic Asylum, which later became Trenton State before being renamed Trenton

Psychiatric Hospital was another facility based on the Kirkbride plan. The hospital was founded by Dorothea Dix and for a time worked as it was meant to in order to help patients, but it was also the site of horrific experimentation. Dr. Henry Cotton was the director of the hospital starting in 1907. At first, all seemed normal and he believed in occupational therapy, increasing the staff, and made sure nurses would prevent violence. They had daily staff meetings to talk about patient care.

However, Dr. Cotton started developing a theory about mental disorders, which turned the lunatic asylum from a place of good into what is remembered as a place of horror. In 1913, spirochaete was found to cause syphilis, which can also lead to psychiatric symptoms. Cotton, reading of this new discovery, started to theorize that all mental illnesses could be caused by infections of the body, and the only way to cure the patient was to treat the infection. Four years later, he started removing patient's teeth even when the x-rays did not show infection. He also started removing other body parts like the gall bladder, ovaries, stomach, testicles, uterus, and parts of the colon from patients as a means of treating illness. Cotton even claimed he cured 85% of his patients. What was actually going on was a high mortality rate and most often without the consent of the family members or patients. Dr. Henry Cotton was not silent on his experiments either. He published several papers about his work. What makes this all the more horrific is that Cotton remained in the position until 1930, just three years before his own death. His theory and practice of pulling teeth remained in use until 1960.

The asylum still stands with the place still being used as a psychiatric hospital although portions of the place are abandoned and in horrible disrepair.

Topeka State Hospital

While not as shocking as some of the other true stories above, the Topeka State Hospital in Kansas has its own gruesome tale. In the early 20th century a reporter went to the facility. During the visit the reporter saw a patient who was strapped down for so long the skin had begun to form over the restraints. Others were recorded as being chained naked for months at a time. Most patients just sat in rocking chairs with no activities or anything to do. Luckily, in 1948, after hearing the reports of untenable conditions and overcrowding, the governor stepped in to improve the hospital, which turned a place of mundane life into one that was considered a leading facility of the day. It is a closed hospital now, having lost funding in the 80s and eventually having to close in 1997.

There are other facilities that could be discussed, but the chapter should have made it clear by now that even well into the 1900s lunatic asylums were nothing more than prisons of horror. Doctors supposedly trained on taking care of patients sometimes developed theories that led to horrific experiments, while others simply did not care to provide treatment. In the next chapter some of the more chilling experiments that went on in asylums will be discussed in detail as a way to examine how experiments in asylums lead to the adoption of treatment as the cure all for mental illness.

Chapter 4: Experiments Conducted in Asylums

The Asylums mentioned in chapter 3 were primarily a place of neglect, but some had the beginnings of the horrific experiments that were considered appropriate and even necessary. Two experiments will be discussed in this chapter: lobotomy and electroshock therapy. This is not to say that more weren't conducted, but these are two of the more horrific concepts the world created and used well into the late 20th century.

Lobotomy

Lobotomy or prefrontal lobotomy was based on the prefrontal lobe. It was suggested in a research study that removing this area of the brain would correct mental illness. Rather than correct the behavior it often left patients to wander. They would not know who they were a lot of the time, and sometimes the experiments actually left the patient in worse behavioral condition than when they went in.

The prefrontal lobe is known for its management of behavior. Damage to the front of the brain can lead to a change in behavior for a person. For example, if someone is in a car accident and their prefrontal lobe is damaged, their behavior, speech, and abilities to care for themselves can change dramatically. Someone with dementia, whose brain shrinks, will change in behavior and speech. A person who was never violent can become violent if that area of the brain is damaged. Inhibitions can suddenly disappear, and the thoughts a person normally would not utter might suddenly come out even though it is not considered appropriate.

It was by study that the behavioral changes due to injury to the prefrontal lobe were discovered. Many doctors listening to patient's family talk of their family member changing after an accident to the front portion of their brain began to record information and conduct long term studies on these patients. Eventually it was suggested that brain surgery on the prefrontal lobe might be able to cure patients of these improper behaviors.

Of course the thought was mainly that by removing the damaged area the patient would again return to their normal self. What happened instead was a complete shutdown of a patient's ambition. By removing the portion of brain that has to do with behavior, most patients lost the will to do much but wander. Their brain was also affected in speech, so talking was something that was difficult or impossible to do.

Despite how inhumane and wrong the concept of lobotomies was at the time, the surgeries were used frequently. Doctors would remove a portion of the brain of any patient that showed violent behavior. It was one way for psychopaths to get treatment. Lobotomies were also used on psychotic and schizophrenic patients.

For directors and doctors at asylums, the treatment was considered successful because the patients were no longer exhibiting the behavior and speech patterns that led them to be institutionalized, but now the world knows differently.

Electroshock Treatment

Electroshock therapy was at times horrific. Like lobotomies there were those who felt shocking the brain would reset the nerves providing signals to a person and change their behavior from crazy to sane. For some patients this was perhaps a true cure. Studies are showing now that schizophrenic patients could have a nerve disorder in the brain. It is related to an inhibitor chemical in the brain that blocks the nerve from functioning as it should. While it is unknown right now if a simple shock could correct the issue, back when electroshock therapy was thought to be highly successful some people were "cured." It might be that the shock to the brain was enough to reset nerves to function properly.

However, just because a certain degree of success was found does not mean all patients and all methods were the same. Every patient subjected to electroshock therapy was mistreated because of misunderstanding mental illness. Some of the patients simply needed care and love rather than an electric pulse sent into their body by the brain. In fact, most of the patients just needed proper care and understanding. Those who exhibited worse symptoms required more care, but through neglect and inhumane treatment did not receive what was needed.

Electroshock therapy machines had a range of electricity that could be chosen for the procedure. A mild shock could be given or something that would shake the entire body leaving the patient nothing more than brain dead. A lot of the patients who underwent electroshock therapy were like those suffering a lobotomy—they would wander, be unable to speak, and stare vacantly at nothing.

Depending on the level of shock, a patient might wake up from their state of stupor to be seemingly cured, or the patient might revert back to their behavior. It all depended on the mental illness or disability the patient was truly suffering from. Mentally handicapped individuals could not control their behavior and thus no amount of shock could help. Electroshock therapy was a favorite for individuals of sexual deviance, whether it was a person who liked the same sex or enjoyed the act of sexual intercourse. Today we are more tolerant, but even into the mid-1900s sexual deviance was treated with electroshock therapy. It is a hypocritical concept too considering asylums like Fernald State School, which would sexually abuse the children who were enrolled for being mentally retarded.

Most of the machines were meant to provide shocks to the brain along the temple. Either patches or a round "crown" would be placed on the patient's head to provide the shock, but there were some very gruesome people offering treatment. These were the psychopaths able to experiment and torture victims because they would take devices and secure them to the eyelids, upper and lower, of the patient to provide a shock around the eyes. Rather than treating the patient properly, these nasty doctors supplied burns around the eyes to patients who would have no other recourse than to act "sane" if they wanted to escape more torture.

While the focus has been on two of the experiments that were once considered the normal way to address mental illness, there are many other treatments and horrific experiments conducted on people for the sake of medicine.

Chapter 5: Movement from Unethical to Ethical Treatments

The 1960s and 1970s were two very important decades, not only for psychology but for the world and its tolerance. The concept of "free love" was perhaps the most important to changing how people viewed the world. This is not to say that certain things have improved, but overall it seemed to mark a time when unethical procedures in hospitals and psychiatric treatment started to turn for more ethical concepts.

During the late 1960s many governors and even the President of the USA started making policies based on the concept of human rights. Already human rights for certain people existed, but a push for all people to have the same human rights was finally beginning. More and more people were beginning to realize that neglect and torture was not the proper way to treat mental illness.

Finally, state facilities and asylums were getting inspected properly and when inhumane treatment was found the facilities were cited, some closed down, and finally a system of checks and balances was put in place.

Prior to the change from unethical to ethical, it was thought that mental disorders had to be hidden away. Even patients with dementia and Alzheimer's were abandoned to facilities and not "talked about" when families were getting together. A person simply disappeared when they were institutionalized. Sometimes the person would be released, considered cured, and re-enter the family but their time away was not discussed.

While neglect on the part of family members has not ended even in this new millennium, at least the mental institutions and "asylums" of today are more tolerant. There is more care in hiring individuals to take care of the mentally ill, mentally challenged, and aging individuals.

Any facility that houses patients, today, is subject to frequent state inspections. If a complaint is made on a facility, then inspectors must go out and view the facility. During the inspection, if there is something cited, then multiple and frequent inspections are made until the facility will pass. For years a facility can be subject to inspections should there be something found.

There is finally a system that will not ignore the mistreatment of others, but it is not perfect. Within the confines of any institution including those for mental disorders there can be improper hiring, neglect, "angels of death," and psychopaths. It takes time to notice when a person is not properly suited for the mental health care profession. The smart individuals are able to hide their torture and neglect of patients. But it is on a smaller degree.

What most places face today is not unethical treatment, but simple lack of caring. Not every person that goes through medical or psychological training to help in mental institutions is right for the job. Unfortunately with a growing number of patients seeking treatment in and out of facilities, it is difficult to keep up with the demand. It means that sometimes neglect happens purely because there are not enough professionals with the proper bedside manner to truly care and help the patient.

Ethical Treatment through Analysis and Therapy

The change in mental institutions to become more ethical also helped the concept of psychoanalysis therapy, occupational therapy, and cognitive therapy to flourish. Today patients are given ethical treatment that focuses on talking and creating a mental health plan with steps for correcting the anxiety, fear, or illness a patient suffers from.

In an outpatient treatment, the person has to be willing to seek treatment. The person will usually seek counseling or therapy from a psychologist or psychiatrist where discussions of the problem occur. The patient may focus on the incident that has caused their mental illness or talk about their entire life as a means of finding the confidence and solution. With outpatient therapy the person is usually given "homework" that maps their behavior patterns such as when they feel anxious or stress, how they could better react in the situation, and eventually how they can ensure the reaction is within normal ranges. It is about a step-by-step plan to ensure the goal is reached.

This is just a small overview of the treatment plans created based on psychoanalysis and therapy. It is just meant to show that changes in thought have occurred and there are more ethical ways to treat mental illness. It is also an alternative to drug therapy.

Drug Therapy

Along with the advent of mental institutions was the concept of drug therapy. Like the abuse of people through tortuous procedures like lobotomy, there were also psychiatrists who firmly believed in medications as the answer to successful mental health treatment. It is through medical experimentation of drugs that we have over 100 different medications that fit two categories: antidepressants and antipsychotics.

Some professionals felt and still feel that a higher dose of medication to suppress the mental illness is necessary. A dose that will end the fear, stress, and anxiety of a patient so that their behavior is not going to be harmful to themselves or others has long been a premise of treatment.

To a degree it does work. A patient with suicidal thoughts taking medication can stop the depression and suicidal thoughts. They can then be treated with therapy to ensure the problem is corrected. Of course the patient can be just as likely to attempt suicide or succeed at it with the medications, because a side effect of some antidepressants is actually an increase in suicidal thoughts.

Antipsychotics are designed to help reduce hallucinations and delusions. Like antidepressants the theory is to medicate to control the behavior so the patient can undergo therapy to correct their overall beliefs.

The trouble with drug therapy is dependency. Some patients develop a dependency for the drugs and are never able to let them go. Others need to remain on the medications even in small doses to ensure self-harm or violence against others does not occur.

It takes time and patience for the patients to be monitored and helped. It also takes the patient submitting to long-term treatment for it to work. While more ethical treatments exist, there are still issues within the mental health community that have yet to be solved. Some find it is easier to prescribe medication, leave a patient to be lifeless, and not correct the underlying issues, while others are fully dedicated and the patients are not. Until the proper balance for all mental patients is found, problems will continue to occur.

Chapter 6: Where Psychology is heading Today

The American Psychological Association president wrote a paper in 2009 about the future of psychology, mostly in the realm of practice and treatment. It is this paper that will spark the beginning of a discussion on where psychology is heading today. It is clear from the previous chapters, the history of it all, and the outline of mental institutions and hospitals today that there is still a need for mental health care. In fact, according Dr. James Bray the APA president, the need for care for mental illnesses is on the rise and the 21st century is going to be the millennium that sees positive changes. The traditional way of treating patients is going to evolve because of the advancement of technology, science, and our thought processes.

What history has clearly shown is that we did not have enough understanding or tolerance of difference. Anyone that had "crazy" behavior was seen as a leper of society that needed to be hidden, ignored, and largely mistreated. Even through much of the 20th century treatment was still creating unsavory conditions. This means the new millennium needs to embrace the advances found in the latter 20th century like genetics and DNA.

It does not mean inhumane concepts will go away. Already there is talk of cloning an entire person just to see if it can be done and to better help the understanding of the human body. There are those who would like to experiment on more than mice in a lab to see if their theories work with regards to certain genes and neurological pathways as a means of finding a cure for mental illnesses like schizophrenia and antisocial personality disorders. Luckily human rights and ethical patient treatment are stopping these unethical experiments, but it does not mean science is at a standstill.

According to Dr. Bray, there are four areas that need improvement:

- Public understanding

- Integrating of technology

- Meeting diverse societal needs

- Applying basic and applied scientific evidence into practice

Dr. Bray has a firm belief that mental health professionals need to be more integrated in medicine and science. Psychologists need the basic core classes in science and medicine, but most can forego a full degree. Most mental health professionals are psychologists, meaning they cannot prescribe medications and their studies are on the mind, sociology, and therapy practices versus medical. The medical system needs a full integration of care not only of the human mind in terms of mental health, but also in keeping with medical conditions. According to Dr. Bray, 70% of the mental health general care providers address problems in the USA. A doctor with little psychology training is prescribing medications for depression, PTSD, and other mental illnesses. They do so without any psychologist input. This is dangerous. It has also led to many patients going untreated for proper mental health issues.

For example, a patient with bipolar disorder may be treated for depression. A person with PTSD may be given medication to help with the fear, dreams, and depression, but the mental health or truthfully the root of the problem is not addressed.

The typical primary care physician spends 15 minutes with their patient for any visit, whether it is an annual exam or a checkup for mental health, an existing condition, or for a cold. This means the patient is not actually being cared for in all areas. Research is even suggesting that diabetes, obesity, and heart disease are caused more by mental illness than by genetic predispositions. It means that the person has adopted a lifestyle that is unhealthy due to depression or another type of mental illness.

To change the problem doctors need to be psychologists or at least have psychologists on staff to consult with all patients. A full care option should be offered. Perhaps it would be too much to insist that a new patient of a primary care physician also speak with a psychologist on the first visit, but it is the best way for a patient to realize help is available.

A health exam should include one's mental state given that our behavior and personality directly affect how we live. It is Dr. Bray's opinion that this area must change first before mental health care can improve to a new level.

Integrating Technology

Technology has already been implemented since the 2009 article. There are now electronic health records or HER records as well as other technological advancements that have been made with regards to tracking patient information. Unfortunately, there is still an issue as it is not a national system. There is no one standard developed at the moment. It means that from state to state, even from doctor to doctor the systems are not linked. The reason for implementing technology is for better patient records. A doctor can call up all previous visits to see what has occurred, been discussed, and the health plan of the patient as a means of seeing if any goals have been reached. While it is a nice system, patients still have to transfer those older records to their new doctors.

A part of this is patient confidentiality and protection of the patient's information. It is necessary to have patient rights, but there can be a simpler method to ensuring this happens without compromising the technology concept. A national database could be established, maintained, and provided to health care providers when proper authorization is given. It would mean the physician could have a signed document from the patient, go in and access the national system and download the patient records. It would streamline the process, but as of yet the laws and regulations do not support such an option. Dr. Bray is even satisfied with the EHR system as it stands right now.

Diverse Society Needs

We live in a diverse society. While the world is becoming more globally oriented, there is also a fight by many to keep their nationality and culture alive. This means that society is going to remain ethnically diverse, and psychology still has to find a way to meet the needs of the people. The US census shows that 47 million Americans as of 2009 were without health insurance. This was about 16% of the population. The implementation of the health care marketplace has helped particularly with the threat of penalty for not having health insurance when a person can afford it. States also had the option of correcting their Medicaid and Medicare programs to ensure those in need could still gain health insurance. While health insurance is being taken care of, it doesn't mean that a small percent of the community is going to get the help it needs.

Proper training in volunteer facilities that are sought by impoverished groups is lacking. These facilities are also available on short term hours, meaning that patients cannot always get the help they need when they are most in need. There are also multiple cultures that do not believe in mental health care, which limits the ability for those in need to feel it is okay to seek help.

About the time Dr. Bray wrote his article, there was another study released on psychological disorders and poverty. The study shows that most individuals with a mental disorder like schizophrenia, bipolar, PTSD and other illnesses are homeless, living on the streets, and incapable of getting the care they need. They either do not seek it or are so lost they do not know they need it. This community is still going to be overlooked even with the above two changes being implemented.

Practicing it All

Basic and applied scientific evidence is currently being studied. More research into mental health disorders is occurring. It is a great movement towards supplying the help needed, but there is still a need for the evidence based practice to occur. Graduate students need to learn the proper methods and how to integrate science into psychology and vice versa. Neuroscience for example is a big area of study right now for many mental disorders including psychopath, sociopath, and schizophrenia. Psychologists need to understand this research, implement it in their practices and ensure the community has access to the information too.

Much of the above is just the opinion of the writer and that of Dr. James Bray's information discovered on the APA website. There is certainly ample evidence to suggest that changes need to be made even in 2015. Strides have been made to improve the overall system, but there is much that needs to happen for psychology's future. A part of it is the education of the public.

Take a moment to look over the following questions:

- Do you know someone who has sought psychological help?

- Did you know there are some states that offer a mental health program where a patient without insurance can visit for free up to 4 times a year and seek unlimited group therapy?

- Have you known a patient who was neglected in a mental health or medical institute?

If you answered yes to the above questions, then you are in a low percentage of well informed individuals. If you answered no to the first question, the reason you may not know a person obtained mental health care is because the stigma of mental health still exists. Even today many feel that seeking care for a mental illness is considered a weakness or something to be ashamed of. Psychology professionals and society as a whole has to work on this.

If you answered that you are unaware of state mental health programs, then it means the marketing job of the psychology industry is not working hard enough to help patients or we as society are not paying proper attention. It is of the opinion of this writer that it is both. With the Internet it is possible to find out anything if one wants to seek the information. However, the psychology industry could do better to ensure that free programs are announced in more than just certain areas. If the credit crisis tells us anything, it is the possibility that once affluent residents can become impoverished, jobless, and homeless yet still need mental and medical health care. A person who once afforded mental health care is more likely not to be aware of free help.

Lastly, if you answered that you do not know of any patient that was neglected in either means, your family and friends are extremely healthy or no one talks about it. Neglect still exists in a variety of health care related industries. The difference is we are attempting to fix the problem.

This book has outlined the lack of care, mistreatment, and even the neglect that has led to killers getting away with murder in the name of psychology treatment. It has showed that our intolerance of mental illness and mental handicaps lets us be inhumane. Now neglect is due more to an overwhelming need of many people worldwide. There are more people being diagnosed with mental disorders, dementia, schizophrenia, psychopath personality disorder, bipolar, depression, and health issues. The continued growth of the popular does not help in that respect. But what truly makes it all harder is that there are only a select few who are truly born to care enough about patients to ensure proper care.

Many enter the field with plans to do well, but find they are burned out quickly. The industry does not have enough psychologists and trained professionals on hand to cover the growing number of mental illness diagnosis, let alone those who leave because they burn out quickly.

Most people know of at least one person in their family tree or friend's family tree that has been mistreated or neglected in their care, but do little about it. So while the horrors of extreme mistreatment are corrected, the psychology industry has a ways to go for a better future.

Printed in Great Britain
by Amazon

86066380R00027